Bι

Helping Kids Overcome Anxiety

By

Mo Mydlo

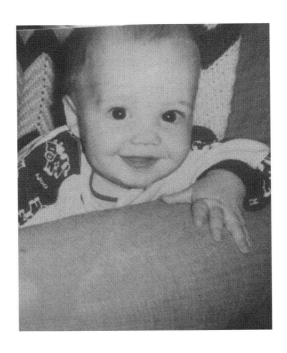

Dedication

The book is dedicated to my precious nieces and nephews. God has truly given me such joy watching you all grow up. I thank God for all of your hearts. Each and every one of you are precious in God's sight. I pray that you are enriched by this book and that it helps those of you who are just a little bit like Aunt Mo Mo. I hope you enjoy seeing your precious smiles all over this book. I love you abundantly and so does Jesus.

Acknowledgments

I have to thank God first and foremost for spoon feeding me each lesson. I thank you for not allowing me to rush, as the next Joy Builder was coming right around the corner. I thank you for showing me when you were finished speaking and that I needed to get submitting. I love you, Lord. You are my King!

I want to thank Tommy and the kids, Jake, Travis, Sara and Eli for understanding when mama had to just shut her door and get typing. I thank you for loving me through anxious moments when I ask a lot of questions to make sure you are okay. I want to thank you all for loving me like Jesus loves me. You five people will have my heart for eternity. I thank God every day that you all know Him intimately and that not even death can keep us from each other, as we will all live with Jesus someday.

I want to thank my parents and Tommy's parents for always supporting me in whatever God calls me to do. I want to thank my Pastor, Jason Hitte, for encouraging my writing and teaching and never questioning the call on my life. I want to thank my dear friends the Petersons for always believing in the ministries that we serve in together on a daily basis.

I want to thank my friends with little worriers at home who have been patient with me as I write this and have encouraged me to keep going. It is my prayer that God blesses your home with peace and joy and eradicates your children's anxiety once and for all, in Jesus' name.

Introduction for the Parents or Loved Ones of Our Little Overcomers

How Does This Study Work?

This is an interactive study between parents or loved ones and their child. The goal of this study is to help children learn behavioral techniques, habits and life skills that will help them to become overcomers of anxiety once and for all.

 It is written as a bedtime bible study. No matter the age of the child, I would like the study to be read to the child, not encouraged to be read on their own. I did this specifically to create healthy, happy memories between children and their loved ones as they grow in their awareness of why they worry; to teach them how to stop worrying, and to show them how to trust God, first and foremost, with their lives. Together the children and their loved ones reading it to them will grow closer to Jesus as they dig in and study scriptures together each evening.

There is a Share Time each evening. This Share Time is meant to be a safe place where children can put to words the things that are bothering them. When we speak our anxious thoughts out loud, it breaks the strength of the thought. Please keep Share Time confidential for your child. They need to trust you as they share their little hearts.

There is a time of Thanksgiving each night. The children will have to think of three things that they are thankful for. Living a life of thankfulness helps us to keep proper perspective about the things that are bothering us. Make sure you don't skip this step. It is very important.

My prayer is that you enjoy reading to your precious child each night. This study has no time limits. You may choose to focus on one Joy Builder each night for 20 nights, or you can choose to read the same joy builder each night for a week, for a total of 20 weeks doing the study. It's up to you and your little overcomer. Set your own pace by how well you see that your child is comprehending the lessons.

I am not a licensed psychologist. I'm not a doctor. I'm an ordained minister, a mother of four, an aunt, a friend and an overcomer of the anxiety that I have struggled with since childhood. I know a lot about overcoming anxiety only because I have studied it and worked at it my entire life with the Lord. I believe that the best lessons in life are taught by those teachers who have first experienced the test.

I will be praying for you as you engage on this special journey with your child.

Building Joy

Hi, my friend. My name is Mo. I am an author, which means I write books. I have written a few books. One of my favorite books that I have written teaches adults how to overcome anxiety. What is anxiety? Well, anxiety is that feeling we get that something scary might happen. Anxiety is that feeling we feel when everything seems to be okay, but we are just nervous it won't always be.

Anxiety is an emotion. God made us with emotions, but anxiety isn't an emotion that He wants us to feel. God actually wants us to feel peaceful, happy and safe. God wants us to trade our emotion of anxiety in for a good emotion as soon as we start to feel it. Sounds tricky, right? Trading in emotions for other emotions. Let me explain. It's not that tricky and also makes us feel so much better. I want to help you to learn how to do that. Will you let me teach you?

How do I know how to do this? Because I have been fighting the feeling of anxiety, or I should say fear, since I was a little child, like you. Therefore, I know how you feel. Does that make you feel a little better? I know it would me. Just to know someone else feels like you do. Sometimes when I was younger I would look around and everyone else seemed so happy. I wanted to feel happy, but something was always making me feel nervous. I always felt responsible for things I didn't do that were wrong. I always wanted to fix whatever wasn't perfect. I always wanted to protect myself and others from any kind of pain. I always was afraid of something going wrong. Do you feel like that sometimes? If you do, I bet you often wish you could feel more peaceful. Am I right?

Does nighttime scare you? It used to scare me. I used to hate when the lights were out because I didn't like to think about all of the dangerous things that were in the dark. But, guess what? I'm not afraid of the dark anymore. I have learned that God is with me in the dark and the light and that He has special angels that sit by me at my bedside to protect me. Guess what? You also have angels protecting you. God's Word tells us that.

I wanted to write this book, "Building Joy" for you because I felt Jesus tell me that He loves children so much He wants them to be happy, healthy and peaceful. I sure do love Jesus. He is the most special person in my life and He wants to be the most special person in your life. Do you know Him?

Jesus is God's son. God sent His son to earth because in the beginning Adam and Eve, (the first people on earth) sinned. (That means, they did something to go against God's laws). After Adam and Eve sinned, everyone born after them, were born with sin in their hearts. That is the reason why we sometimes do bad things.

God sent Jesus as a baby to grow up and show us how not to sin. He lived among us for about 30 years, taught people how to love others, healed the sick, fed hungry people, made lonely people feel not so lonely, and did good things wherever He went. Then, when Jesus was about 33 years old, He was nailed to a cross and died. But the amazing news is that He came back to life three days later. He rose from the dead! When He did this, He broke the power of sin in our lives. This may be confusing, I know; but the best part is, after we learn about what Jesus did for us and we believe it and we begin to trust Him with our lives, we are guaranteed a ticket into Heaven someday when we die. We never have to worry about dying ever again because when we take our last breaths here on earth, we get to live FOREVER with Him in Heaven because we have made Jesus our friend.

What is Heaven? It is where God our Father lives, and Jesus and His angels and many of our Grandmas and Grandpas and family members live there because they knew Jesus. The Bible describes Heaven as a place with streets made of pure gold, a place where no one ever cries because there is no sadness, tears or anything bad in Heaven. Heaven is perfect. Heaven is amazing. Heaven is where we go when we die because we love and follow Jesus. God works each day preparing a place for us someday there. He really is amazing.

I know, you love your parents and loved ones and family more than anyone else. I don't blame you. But, guess what? Someday, after you meet Jesus, you will love Him even more than them. Can you believe that? It surprised me too, when I first met Him.

How do you meet Jesus? Well, it really isn't that complicated. Jesus is just waiting for you to meet Him and make Him the Lord of your life. It's a prayer, and I can pray it with you right now. Do you want to?

Ok, close your eyes and you can say this prayer with me to Him:

"Jesus, I'm sorry that I have made mistakes in my past..." (Now, you)

"I thank you that you died on the cross for my mistakes that are called sins..." (Now, you)

"I thank you that I don't have to worry about those mistakes because you died so I could have peace..." (Now you)

"Jesus, I believe that you died on the cross and three days later rose from the dead..." (Now, you)

"I want to follow you for the rest of my life..." (Now, you)

"Come into my life, come into my heart and fill me with your Holy Spirit..." (Now, you)

"Jesus, you are Lord! I love you..." (Now, you)

"Amen" (Now, you)

I'm so happy for you. You are now a friend of Jesus just like me. You are now a believer in Jesus and what the Bible talks about as a disciple. A disciple follows Jesus. A disciple tries to live like Jesus. How do we know how Jesus lived? We read His Bible. We read all about the great things He did while He lived here on earth.

Do you have a Bible? If not, ask mommy and daddy or someone you love to get you one. You can buy them pretty much anywhere, or most churches will give you one for free. The Bible is what we are going to learn to read together to help you not worry about things anymore. Did you know that the Bible can do that? Oh my goodness, the Bible is amazing. It is like God's love letter to us. He wrote it to us to let us know how much He loves us.

Do you know God loves you? If you don't know that, I'm very excited to be the first person to tell you God loves you. God loves you so much that He sent Jesus to earth to die for us because we were sinners and, as sinners, it wasn't easy to be God's friend. He wants us to be His friends. He loved Jesus so much that He sacrificed Him for us, because God also loves us like that. He wants us to be in Heaven with Him someday, and He also wants us to be able to talk to Him every day through prayer while we live here on earth.

Do you know that you can talk to God through prayer? What is prayer? Prayer is simply talking to God. You can pray silently or out loud. God hears both. It doesn't have to be fancy. You can tell him or ask Him anything you want. He really is awesome. Prayer is another amazing tool that helps us not to be anxious or scared. When we are afraid, we can just talk to God and the next thing we know, we aren't afraid anymore. It really is something that humans can't understand. It's what we call, "a God thing." Prayer is one of the tools we need as Christians to live in peace and joy and protection. Prayer is powerful, and when you pray angels go to work to try to help you. Isn't that cool?

Well, we've learned about Jesus, the Bible, prayer and what it means to be a Christian, or another word to call it, a disciple. I want to discuss one more thing. It's called baptism. In the Bible when people decided to follow Jesus, they got baptized. Baptism is a ceremony done at church or in a lake or a pool. Baptism represents the fact that we truly believe Jesus was born, lived, died on the cross and that God raised Him from the dead. We actually go under water and come right back up. When we do that, it's a symbol of Jesus dying and coming back to life. It's called immersion.

After you start following Jesus, I hope you will find a church to go to and let them know you want to be baptized. The pastor (the teacher at the church) will probably ask you a few questions about when you decided to follow Jesus and if you understand it. After he answers any questions you may have, then you can be baptized. It's a beautiful way to show the world that you are a new follower of Jesus Christ. Remember a follower of Jesus Christ is called a Christian or a disciple. Christians follow Jesus. Since Jesus was baptized in the Bible, we get baptized. We should always try to do the things that Jesus did. It's truly a great way to live. Pray about it with your parents or with someone you love. They will help you take your next steps.

Wow! This is a lot right? I'm really excited, because you might be another brand new believer tonight just from reading the beginning of this book. That makes me smile because I may meet you here on earth, one day. But if not, someday we may meet in Heaven because we both love Jesus now. Are you excited about that too?

You want to hear something else that excites me? Maybe Mommy or Daddy or whoever is reading this to you hasn't made Jesus their Lord yet and they need to pray that prayer. Ask them! If they say they have never made Him Lord of their life, then I hope they decide right now to make Him their best friend as well. You can both get to know Him together. You see, Jesus wants everyone to be with Him someday in Heaven. Not just children, everyone!

If you were already a Christian when you picked up this book, then thank you for being patient with our new brothers and sisters in Christ, because now we are all on the same page and can start talking about no more worrying! Are you excited about that? Me too. It feels good to just have shared the best gift ever given (Jesus) with our new friends, doesn't it?

Here's how the book works, Mommies and Daddies or someone that loves you (who I call your "loved one") will read it to you. This way, they can answer questions that you may have and they can explain things you don't understand. Also, they can pray with you. I'm so excited about happy and healthy memories being made together. Are you excited for them to read this to you? I am! I used to love when people I loved read to me. Now I love reading to my kids. It's going to be great!

Each topic will be called a Joy Builder. After you finish a Joy Builder, there are questions you can talk over together. After you talk about the questions, there will be a Share Time. You get to share whatever you want with your loved one reading to you. This is a safe place. It's a time to be real. What do I mean to "be real"? I mean, don't bottle up what you want to talk about. You need to let it out. God said to me one time, "You have to be real to be healed." Your loved one reading this to you wants you to be happy and joyful and full of peace. Don't be afraid to share whatever God puts on your heart. They can handle whatever you talk about. So, let it fly! Let me tell you a secret. My husband is who I have Share Time with when I get worried about something. I pray and give it to Jesus, then I sometimes tell my husband, because just saying it out loud to someone else sometimes makes us feel so much better, no matter what it is.

After Share Time, we have to have Thanksgiving Time. No, not Thanksgiving dinner. We can't eat turkey and stuffing every day. Thanksgiving Time is going to be the time each night that we say thanks to God for at least three things. You can say anything. You could be thankful for your parents or for your dog. Some nights, you may feel thankful for your pens and pencils you take to school. Whatever your three things are each night is up to you.

Sometimes there are blanks to fill in, so make sure you have a pencil, pen, crayon or marker ready, (whichever is your favorite) to use. I have pens that look like flowers. They make me happy. How about you?

We are going to learn scriptures by saying them out loud together, then there will be a prayer focus. We will pray together. Then you can go to bed expecting to have great dreams because you have grown in Christ, talked about what is bothering you, prayed it out to God and done all of this with someone you love. What could be better than that? I'm so happy for you.

You can do as many Joy Builders each night as you like. If you and your loved one are having fun and you want to keep going onto more Joy Builders, go for it! Some nights, you might not even make it through a whole Joy Builder and it might take you a few nights. That's ok. You also could choose to do a Joy Builder once a week and work through it all week. It's your decision and this is your bible study and your special time getting closer to Jesus.

Do you have your jammies on? Did you brush your teeth? Then okay, let's get started building more joy in our lives and learning how to not have anxiety! I'm praying for you. It's going to be great.

Joy Builder #1

Learning Not to Worry Takes Time

"Faith comes by hearing and hearing by the Word of God." Romans 10:17

We like things fast, don't we? We like to go through the drive- thru at our favorite restaurant and get our chicken nuggets and fries and chocolate milk. We don't love waiting too long. Waiting can be tough. My mom used to say, "Patience is a virtue." I didn't always know what that meant, but she always seemed to say it to us when we were being really impatient as kids. It's hard to wait, right?

God knows we hate to wait, but for some reason when we are trying to learn how not to worry, it takes a while. Do you want to know why? Because we have to learn new things. We have to learn God's Word. We have to learn how to realize that if a thought is not a good thought that God would want us thinking, we have to decide to stop thinking about it. We have to learn how to pray and wait for God's answers to our questions. We have to learn how to grow our faith in God's ability to handle ALL of our problems. We have to learn how to trust God, when sometimes we struggle even trusting people that we can see. All of these things that we have to learn won't happen overnight. We have to pace ourselves, like runners in a long race when they don't want to run out of energy or breath.

This scripture says, "Faith comes by hearing and hearing by the Word of God." That means the more we hear the Word of God and the more we read the Word of God, the more faith we will have. Therefore, we need to read and listen to the Bible. We listen to it by reading out loud. Even though in school we have to read quietly to ourselves so that we don't disturb others, when at home reading our Bibles, it's really good to read it out loud. Since faith comes by hearing, it's good to hear ourselves reading the Bible, so we can grow our faith.

Why do we need to grow our faith? As our faith grows, our fears shrink. The more we realize that Jesus can handle any of our problems, fears or worries, the less we will be scared.

---

*Can you say our scripture out loud with me? "Faith comes by hearing..." (Now, you) And hearing, by the Word of God"... (Now, you) Romans 10:17.

*Great job! Say it two more times with your loved one reading with you.

*How can you spend more time reading and hearing God's Word?

*When can you make more time in your day to stop and just have a talk with Jesus (pray)?

*Share Time: Talk about whatever you are thinking about.

*Thanksgiving Time! Thank God for three things. Whatever three things you can think of.

*Prayer Focus: Pray with your loved one about anything that you shared that maybe you want to share with Jesus, then ask God to make you want to read His Word (the Bible) more.

Let me pray for you. Dear God, in the name of Jesus, bless my friend. Help my friend to sleep sweetly. Help my friend to pray to you more, read Your Word more and grow my friend's faith. In the name of Jesus, amen! Good night, friend! I love you.

Joy Builder #2

Learning to Trust God

"Trust in the Lord with all of your heart and lean not on your own understanding; in all of your ways acknowledge Him and He will direct your path." Proverbs 3:5-6

What does "trust" mean? Well, trust is all about believing. Think about your chair or bed that you are sitting on right now. Unless it is broken, you trust that it is going to hold you up, right? You aren't worried that you may fall on the floor, are you? Well, that's because your bed or chair has always held you, so you can trust it always will, or you believe it always will. That's what trusting means.

God wants us to trust Him with everything, especially our hearts. (Our hearts you may know as the organ that beats to keep us alive.) Yes, that is true because God made our hearts to work so that we will be healthy and stay alive. But this scripture that says; "trust in the Lord with all of our heart..." means; to trust God with everything in our lives.

We need to trust God with our mommys, daddys, sisters, brothers, cousins, homes, our schoolwork, our pets, our friends, and everything we can think of.

If we can learn to trust God with everything, we won't worry. Here is what I mean. You know that little thought that comes into our minds that says, "What if?" Our minds say, "What if this happens? What if that happens? What if, what if, what if?" Do you know what I mean?

Well, I want you to learn that whenever that voice comes into your head and says, "What if?" You respond out loud or to yourself saying, "I trust God." Say that right now. "I trust God." Yes, I trust God too. Do you know why? Because He has never let me down. He won't. Anytime I pray, the Bible tells me He hears me, so, I can pray to Him about anything, and He always hears.

Sometimes people let us down because they are human. Humans aren't perfect and they disappoint us. We disappoint other people. We will never be perfect, but God is perfect. We can trust Him with anything that we are thinking about.

Let's learn how to trust in The Lord with ALL of our heart.

*Say this out loud with your loved one: "Trust in the Lord, with all of your heart." (Now, you)

*Great. Now say it out loud two more times.

*Write down a few things that you want to learn to trust God with.

1.

2.

3.

4.

5.

6.

7.

I know you probably have so many more. Great job! I'm proud of you.

*What are you going to say the next time you have a "What if?" thought?

*Share Time

*Thanksgiving Time! Thank God for three things. Whatever three things you can think of.

*Prayer Focus: Pray for all of the things and people you listed that you want to trust God with.

Now let me pray for you: Dear Heavenly Father, we come to you in Jesus' name. Bless my friend. Allow my friend to trust you with everything, and I mean everything. Lord, give my friend a great night's sleep and peaceful dreams. In Jesus' name, amen.

Good night, friend! I love you.

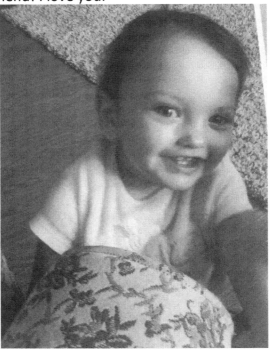

Joy Builder #3

Why Me, God?

"I praise you because I am fearfully and wonderfully made; your works are wonderful,

I know that full well."

Do you ever look around and think, "why don't these other people look like they are worried about things? Why do they always seem happy and peaceful?" I know I used to think that too. I would go to a party that is supposed to be fun, but something would be bothering me, so I couldn't enjoy myself. Has that ever happened to you?

I know this all feels unfair. However, I want to tell you a secret. Everyone has something in their life that makes them feel empty. Everyone struggles with something. Maybe other people that you know don't have anxiety, but they may have a problem with something else like their health. Or maybe another person that you know who is healthy but has a hard time understanding schoolwork. Or you may have a friend that struggles with stuttering or difficulty with their speech.

You see, everyone has something that makes them unique and in need of some help from Jesus. I call this their "God-shaped hole" that is in their heart. God made each of us in His image. We are beautifully and wonderfully made, with one small area, seen or unseen, that requires some extra attention from Him. Anxiety has always been my God-shaped hole. It is the part of me that will always require Jesus' help so I can live in peace.

Guess what? I think God does this on purpose so we will spend more time with Him. He allows us to be imperfect so we can run after Him. He is perfect, and He can help us with our imperfections. Anxiety is not my only imperfection, but it is the one thing that God uses to pull my heart towards Him and make me fall in love with Him.

Oh yes, I love Jesus. I need Jesus. I wouldn't want to go one second without Jesus as my best friend and Savior. He has filled my God-shaped hole with His love and peace. I promise He wants to fill up yours. Will you let Him?

*Let's practice this scripture: "I praise you because I am fearfully and wonderfully made." (Now, you) "Your works are wonderful, I know that full well." (Now, you)

*Great job, now say it two more times with your loved one.

*Do you sometimes feel empty and alone?

*Did you know that our emptiness can be filled with Jesus' love? Doesn't that make you feel happy already?

*Share Time!

Thanksgiving Time! Thank God for three things. Whatever three things you can think of.

*Prayer Focus: Pray about whatever you shared, then specifically ask God to send Jesus' love to fill up your God-shaped hole. Thank God for making you perfectly.

*Now, let me pray for you. Dear Lord Jesus, we love you so much. You are such a great Savior. Thank you for filling our God-shaped hole in our hearts with your love. Your love is enough for us and we thank you for it. Lord, I pray for my friend to have an amazing night's sleep filled with joy. In Jesus' name I pray, amen.

Good night, friend. I love you.

Joy Builder #4

Cast Your Cares

"Cast all your anxiety on him because he cares for you." 1 Peter 5:7

Have you ever been fishing? My favorite part about fishing isn't catching fish, it's casting the fishing line out on the water. You hold the button, or grab in the right place depending on the pole, and you pull back your arm and throw it forward carefully to send your hook and bait right where you think there are fish to be caught. Sometimes our timing is off and we hold the button too long, or we get a knot in the line and it doesn't go exactly where we want it to. The best part is that you get to just cast it back out there again as many times as you need to until you get it right where you want. Yes, casting is my favorite part.

Why? Well, I love letting go of the button and trusting the line to do what it is supposed to. It makes an awesome sound and it is really pretty going across the water. Do you know that in the Bible it says to cast our anxiety on Jesus because he cares for us? Well, if you understand fishing, you understand what that would look like. It would require taking whatever is bothering you, throwing it out of your brain and into Jesus' arms, letting Him take it from you so you don't have to carry it anymore.

Do you think you could do that? Do you think that the next time something is bothering you, such as a test that you are nervous about taking or maybe worrying about something that is physically making you feel bad in your body or maybe a worry about your parents or a loved one, you could take it and cast it on Jesus? I bet you could.

Let me show you a trick. Take your hand and open it up. Place your hand on your head. Come on, don't feel silly, I'm doing it too. Take your hand, put it on your head like you are taking your worry out of your head and putting it into your palm. Now close your fist. Picture that thought now in your fist and not in your brain anymore. Now pretend Jesus is standing in front of you playing catch. Toss it to Him. Go ahead, toss it like you are out at baseball practice. Toss Jesus that thought like you would cast a fishing line out on the lake.

Now, say, "Thank you Jesus, I'm casting my care on you." (Your turn. Go ahead and say it as you toss it.) Great! Do it again just to practice.

Now, the biggest thing we need to remember is, do not take it back from Jesus. He tells us in His Word to give Him our anxiety (which is our fears and worries) because He cares about us. We need to obey Him and throw it to Him and not take it back.

How do we take it back? Well, if you start thinking about it again, you are taking it back. Don't do that! Jesus wants you to feel free. He doesn't want you worrying. He wants you to have fun and be happy and just be a kid. Worrying isn't for you. Let Jesus take it, and don't take it back.

Remember when I said that if you cast the line out and you don't get it right where you want it, you can keep re-casting? Well, it's the same with casting our cares on Jesus. If you catch yourself thinking about it again, don't feel bad, just put your hand on your head again, put the worry in your fist and toss it to Jesus and say, "Thank you, Jesus. I'm casting my care on you."

Guess what? You will not believe how good it feels. You will begin to enjoy your days more, you will have better dreams and you will be able to focus more on what you should be thinking about; such as your schoolwork, or sports or whatever you are doing that day.

I promise, you'll get the hang of it. Please practice it next time you get nervous. It's called casting your cares. Pretty soon you will get so good at it that the second a worry starts, you will just say, "Thank you, Jesus. I'm casting my cares on you" and you can just picture yourself handing it to Jesus and you won't even need to do the throw. You are going to get that good at this. I'm sure of it.

Great job!

---

*Let's practice saying this scripture together: "Cast all your anxiety on Him (Now, you) because He cares for you." (Now, you) 1 Peter 5:7

*Nice Job. Now say it two more times with your loved one.

*What would be an example of a worry or fear that you would cast onto Jesus?

*Do you sometimes not know what to do with a thought that is bothering you, like you wish you had somewhere to put it?

Well, now you do. In Jesus' loving arms.

*Share time!

*Thanksgiving Time! Name three things that you are thankful for.

*Prayer Focus: First pray to Jesus about anything that you shared with your loved one that you would like to cast into Jesus' loving arms. Now, thank Him for taking care of all of your needs.

Let me pray for you: "Heavenly Father, we come to you in Jesus' name and we thank you. God, you are so good that you sent us Jesus so that we don't have to carry our own worries. We can make them into a ball and cast them like a fishing line right into Jesus' arms. Thank you, Jesus for carrying all of our fears. We love you. Bless my friend and help my friend to have sweet, peaceful sleep tonight. In Jesus' name, amen.

Good night friend! You are getting really good at this joy thing! I'm proud of you. I love you.

Joy Builder #5

Out of Our Heads and Onto Paper

"Do not be anxious about anything, but in every situation, by prayer and petition, with thanksgiving, present your requests to God."
Philippians 4:6

Do you like to keep a diary? I used to love to write in my diary when I was little and lock it with the little key that belonged to it. I know my sister used to sneak a peek at it because she was really good at finding my key, but I didn't care. I would still write my secrets in there. Do you have a diary? We also may call it a journal. I keep journals now. I think they are like a grown- up diary. You can write anything you want in it, and it's only for you and God. Yes, sometimes people see our journals, but it's still supposed to be something special between you and Jesus.

You can write your prayers in a journal. I like to do this, and then date it, because sometimes I go through old journals just to see how God has answered my old prayers. It's so fun and it really grows my faith every time I see Jesus' work in my life.

Your journal can also be a place you keep your lists of things you want to do, your future goals, or really anything you want to remember. I like to write down cool things that have happened that day so I don't forget it later.

You know, God keeps his own kind of journal in Heaven. It's called His "book of remembrance." The Bible says this: Malachi 3:16-18: "Then those who feared the Lord spoke to one another, and the Lord gave attention and heard it, and a book of remembrance was written before Him for those who fear the Lord and who esteem His name. 'They will be Mine,' says the Lord of hosts, 'on the day that I prepare My own possession, and I will spare them as a man spares his own son who serves him. So you will again distinguish between the righteous and the wicked, between one who serves God and one who does not serve Him.'" God is so cool, isn't' He? He keeps track of us in His book of remembrance. Don't you think if God keeps a journal, we should? We want to do the things He does, right? We want to be like Jesus, right? I know I do.

Guess what is also really great about journaling? It makes us feel good. When we are worried, we can put our worries in our journal and then, just like how we casted our cares on Jesus (remember our last Joy Builder) and we didn't have to think about them anymore, once we get the worries onto paper, we don't have to keep them in our heads anymore. Whew, that's nice, right? Somedays I can't wait to write my worries in my journal, so I can get them out of my head. Once I write them down I say the same kind of thing I say when I cast my cares on the Lord; "Thank you Jesus, I am giving these cares to you, because you care for me." Once we say the name of Jesus, something powerful happens. We are able to feel peaceful again.

Tonight's scripture reminds us that Jesus does not want us worrying. It reads: "**Do not be anxious about anything, but in every situation, by prayer and petition, with thanksgiving, present your requests to God.**" Philippians 4:6

This scripture is so cool because it specifically tells us; we aren't supposed to worry at all! When Jesus says; "Do not worry about anything." Anything means anything, right?

Then He says; "In every situation, by prayer and petition, with thanksgiving, present your requests to God." In what situations? It says, "In every situation!" That's all the time, my friend. That's every worry, my friend. That's every thought that doesn't make you feel blessed, happy and joyful. The Bible says to present those to God. How do we present them? Well, we can pray them or we can write them in our prayer journals.

Just as we have to remind ourselves not to take our cares back when we toss them into Jesus' hands, we can't take our cares back after we have written them in our prayer journals. You just need to thank Jesus after for taking them from you. This scripture says we have to present them to Jesus with thanksgiving. Well, there it is. Just tell Him thank you. That's all Jesus expects and then He will take it and you don't have to worry about it anymore.

Saying thank you is a good thing to do anyways, right? Well, we need to always tell God thank you. He made us. He loves us. He keeps us safe and secure. That's why we need to always say thank you. We need to tell people thank you when they help us as well. Tell your loved one thank you right now for reading and studying with you. (Go ahead). You can also give them a hug if you want. (I love hugs. They make me smile).

So, I hope you will get yourself a journal. You can use a special book already made that is called a journal, or you can make your own out of loose leaf paper and staples and decorate it yourself and get creative. It doesn't matter what it looks like. It just matters that it is your special prayer journal between you and Jesus. I'm so excited for you. Happy journaling!

---

*Let's say our scripture together. "Do not be anxious about anything. (ok, your turn) but in every situation, by prayer and petition, with thanksgiving, present your requests to God." (I know that's a long one, but you can do it. It's your turn) Philippians 4:6

*Great job! Practice it two more times with your loved one.

*When the Word says, "Do not be anxious about anything," does your latest worry or fear fall under the topic of anything? Is it anything? It is right?

*What does this scripture say to do with the worry?

*What's the important thing that we always should do when Jesus helps us, or someone else helps us?

*Share Time!

*Thanksgiving Time! Thank the Lord for three things!

*Prayer Focus: Pray about anything that you shared that you want to give to Jesus, then tonight just keep thanking God for everything that you can think of that you are grateful for until you are tired of praying. This really is fun to do.

*Let me pray for you: "Dear Lord, thank you for my friend. My friend is working so hard to be a peaceful follower of you. Lord, help my friend to learn how to journal powerfully so that you can take all of my friend's fears away for good. Help my friend to have great dreams. In Jesus' name, amen!

Good night, friend! Great work! I love you.

Joy Builder #6

You Don't Have To Keep Checking

"But when you ask, you must believe and not doubt, because the one who doubts is like a wave of the sea, blown and tossed by the wind. That person should not expect to receive anything from The Lord." James 1:6-7

I used to worry a lot about leaving on the curling iron or the clothes iron and causing a fire. Yes, it is important to make sure that you unplug hot things after you are done with them, but it's not okay to feel like you have to check it over and over and over. Do you know what I mean?

I also used to worry about my tickets and important papers when I would travel or go to an event. Yes, it's important to make sure that you have your tickets, ID and whatever you need to allow for your admission, but it's not okay to feel like you have to check for them over and over and over. Do you ever feel like this?

This sort of checking and rechecking can become an annoying habit of ours when we worry. We can know in our minds that we did something, but when the doubts of "what if I didn't?" creeps in, we can be tempted to check all over again.

These habits are caused by a doubt issue. We have to fight our doubts with trust and faith. I overcame this habit of checking and rechecking things by saying out loud the first time I checked to see if everything was unplugged or where it was supposed to be, "thank you Jesus, it's unplugged," or "thank you Jesus, I have my tickets," or whatever it is you are tempted to check for again. I had to train myself to know that if I told Jesus it was unplugged, then it was unplugged, no matter how quickly the doubt crept into my mind that maybe it wasn't. Do you understand?

You see, this scripture says that we have to ask and then not doubt or we will not get that prayer answered. Well, the truth is doubt happens a lot and we can't feel guilty about it. We simply have to trust God with our doubts. That's why I thank Jesus every time I unplug things or pack important things. This way, when I say the precious name of Jesus, I am placing my doubts in His hands again, and that is the safest place to put anything, in the arms of Jesus.

Tonight, when you go to sleep, instead of thinking, "Did I do this," or "did I do that," if you know you did it, trust! Trust in the beautiful, intelligent, able-minded creature that God made you.

If you know you brushed your teeth, but then you think; "What if I didn't brush my teeth?," practice overcoming doubt by saying; "Thank you Jesus, I brushed my teeth." Then, you can get a great night's sleep believing that your toothpaste and toothbrush will do what they are made to do: fight cavities.

I know this Joy Builder may have seemed silly to you, but it really can be helpful when we start to doubt the things we know in our hearts are true. Doubt is an enemy to faith and we need to be people of faith.

---

*Let's say our scripture together: "But when you ask, you must believe and not doubt." (Okay now your turn.) "because the one who doubts is like a wave of the sea, blown and tossed by the wind." (your turn) "That person should not expect to receive anything from The Lord."(Okay, now, you.)

*Great job. Now say it two more times with your loved one.

*When do you feel tempted to keep checking on things?

*What can you say out loud so that you know that you don't have to check again?

*Share Time!

*Thanksgiving Time!

*Prayer Focus: Spend some time praying about some things that you shared, and then ask God to help you to trust the first time that you check something and say, "Thank you, Jesus, I checked it."

*Okay, now I want to pray for you. Dear Lord, thank you that you are our best friend. Thank you that my friend can put anything that my friend is worried about into your hands and say, "Thank you Jesus. This is yours." Thank you that my friend is learning how not to worry or doubt. My friend is becoming closer and closer to you.

Thank you, Jesus. We love you. Help my friend to have an awesome night's sleep. In Jesus' name, amen.

Good night, my bible study buddy!

I love you!

Joy Builder #7

What is that Voice I Hear?

"You are of God, little children, and have overcome them, because He who is in you is greater than he who is in the world." 1 John 4:4

Do you ever wonder why sometimes you go near something prickly (like a cactus plant) and you think, "What if I touch that?" when you know you don't want to touch it? Or, maybe you walk near the stove or a fire and you hear that voice, "What if you touched this?" when you have heard your mom and dad tell you over and over, never to touch the stove top when it's on and never to get near an open flame? Or, maybe you are going up high in an elevator or an escalator and you think; "what if I leaned too far over? " When, you know you shouldn't. Do you ever get these thoughts? I used to. This little voice used to scare me until I realized what it was. Now, I'm not afraid of that voice anymore. I just had to learn how to get it to stop talking so much.

You see, when we get near something dangerous, God made a little trigger to go off in our brains to remind us that it is dangerous. That trigger tells us, prickly things will poke you if you aren't careful, hot things will burn you if you are not careful and being up very high can be dangerous if you are not careful. This trigger is a good thing. It reminds us of our boundaries. So, don't be afraid of boundaries. Be thankful for them.

Here is where it gets tricky. God designed the trigger to go off to protect us. So, it really is a good thing, but, another little voice comes on the scene from someone who likes to ruin the good things that God designed for us. His name is Satan. Sometimes you may hear people call him the devil. That's another word for him. Satan is a very bad enemy of God's. But, he is no match for Jesus and he is no match for the Holy Spirit who lives on the inside of you now that you are following Jesus. Satan is a liar. All he knows how to do is lie. Unfortunately, Satan tries to lie to you and me, but, we are smarter than Satan. Say out loud right now, "I am smarter than Satan." Good job. Once we realize he is lying to us, we can tell him to leave in the name of Jesus and he has to go, and just like that, you can get back into peace.

When we see something dangerous that we know we shouldn't touch, we need to not touch it and trust our trigger. But, if right after we step away from the danger we keep thinking,"What if I touch it? What if I got too close? What if I do what is bad for me?"or any "what if like that, we know it is the devil (Satan) trying to lie to us and get us worried and afraid. We need to recognize him so that we can kick him out of our brains. Does this make sense?

Really, for those of us who have to work on not being anxious, the two words we need to recognize as two words the devil loves to use is "What if?" Remember, our trigger to stay away from danger is good and we need to obey it (that's from God), but the consistent "What ifs?" after we walk away from the dangers, are not from God, they are from the devil and we can choose to turn them off.

How do we turn them off? With an amazing tool called, The Name of Jesus! Do you know that the Bible says that even the devil has to bow down to the name of Jesus? Do you also know that the Holy Spirit that lives on the inside of you is just as powerful as the name of Jesus? It's so awesome. God truly came to live on the inside of us when we accepted Jesus. When He did that, He gave us the power to tell the devil to shut his voice off.

When that devil says, "What if you did this?" "What if you did that?" "What if you became a bad person?" "What if you make a bad choice"? Have you ever heard these little things whispered in your brain? Well, when he says it to you, you have to talk out loud and tell him to leave. You need to learn to say, "Devil, get out of here in the name of Jesus." Can you say that right now? "Devil, get out of here in the name of Jesus." Great job! I'm proud of you. Don't you feel powerful? Do you know how powerful you are? You are a child of God and children of God are powerful. The Bible explains this in 1 John 4:4. It reads, "You, dear children, are from God and have overcome them, because the one who is in you is greater than the one who is in the world." Isn't that awesome?

We never have to be afraid of Satan. We can listen to our healthy trigger that God gave us to stay out of danger. We can keep the devil from ruining our mood when he tries to whisper his lies to us by saying confidently, "Devil, get out of here in the name of Jesus."

I really enjoy talking to you. I love thinking about how God is going to give you such peace now that you know how much power you have to think about all good things. You are learning so many new things every day. Between school and your Joy Builders, your brain is getting geared up for a successful and happy life. I'm so excited for you.

---

*Let's practice saying our scripture together that we learned tonight; "You dear children, (Now, you) are from God (Now, you) and have overcome them (Now, you) because the one who is in you (Now, you) is greater than the one who is in the world." (Now, you) Nice job!

*Now say it three more times with your loved one.

*What do you need to say out loud when you recognize the devil trying to get you to keep thinking "what if?"

*How do we know if it is our good trigger keeping us from danger or if it is the devil making us worry?

Our trigger tells us once and we obey it, right? The devil is annoying and he tries to keep getting us to worry about it after we listen to our trigger. So tell him to be quiet and let it go.

*Share Time!

*Thanksgiving Time!

Prayer Focus: Spend some time talking to God about some of the things that you shared. Thank God that He gave you your trigger so that you know what is dangerous and what is not and you can stay safe. Thank God that you are powerful and that when the devil tries to steal your joy, you can kick him out like yesterday's trash!

I want to pray for you.

Dear Lord, we come to you in Jesus' name and wow, God, we are so thankful for our triggers. You made us perfectly to protect us from danger. When we know something is unsafe we are able to avoid it because of you, but sometimes when that devil sees that we are listening to our triggers, he tries to jump in and get us worried. Thank you, God that we can tell that devil to leave in the Name of Jesus! Thank you that the name of Jesus is powerful and thank you that we are powerful because of the Holy Spirit inside of us. We love you God. Bless my sweet friend. Help my friend to love you more and more every day. In Jesus' name, amen.

Good night, friend! You are amazing!

Joy Builder #8

You Don't Have To Fix It

"Therefore, there is now no condemnation for those who are in Christ Jesus."

Romans 8:1

Sometimes people argue, right? Does it make you feel uncomfortable? It does me. I remember, when I was little sometimes my parents would argue. I thought I had to figure out a way to get them to stop. I would try to be very good, or clean the house or get in the middle of their argument to try to fix it. I didn't like to hear them fight because it made me nervous. Do you ever do this?

When something happens that doesn't involve you, do you sometimes feel guilty about it anyways? An overactive guilty conscience is a tough thing to deal with. Yes, when I did something wrong, it was good that I felt some shame about it and could change my behavior and not do it again. However, if we feel guilty when other people argue, do something wrong or make mistakes, I believe it makes God sad.

God does not want us feeling guilty about things that we don't do. He doesn't want us to try to fix it. It is not our job to try to fix other people's problems. He doesn't even want us to feel guilty for things that we did do that we have repented for. What does "repented" mean? It means that we have asked for forgiveness and have changed our behavior so we won't do that bad thing again. You see, everyone makes mistakes. Everyone drops the ball sometimes. We can only do our best and give God the rest. So, when we make a mistake and we are truly sorry for it, we have to decide in our minds to let it go for good.

Remember yesterday I told you about Satan? He sure is a bad character. He will sometimes whisper to us that we are supposed to fix things that we cannot fix. He will sometimes whisper to us things to keep making us feel guilty for a long time for things that God (and our parents or teachers or authorities) have already forgiven us for. That devil, Satan doesn't want us to experience peace so he will try to get us feeling very guilty all of the time.

There is a difference between conviction (which is that good voice from God that tells us not to do wrong things) and condemnation (which is Satan trying to steal our joy after we have already repented). Remember, just as I told you yesterday, God's trigger that He has given us is good. It goes off when we are near danger and it even goes off when we are about to do something that we shouldn't. We need to listen to our trigger, but we need to tell the devil to get out! Just like I taught you in Joy Builder #7, my friend, never forget how much power you have in the Holy Spirit that lives on the inside of you. You have the power to experience peace. You have the power to not worry. You have the power to realize that when the devil is trying to trick you, you have the power to make him leave your mind.

Remember that the name of Jesus is powerful. When you start to feel guilty for something that is all over with, or something that really isn't your fault or something that you feel like you have to fix even though you didn't break it, say out loud to yourself, "Devil, leave me alone! God wants me to be in peace! In Jesus' name, leave my mind!" Go ahead and try that now. Great job! You are becoming so strong.

My sweet friend, adults argue from time to time and families sometimes have disagreements and that isn't fun. Sometimes our friends are not nice to us. We have to remember all we can do is our best and give God the rest. God wants us to love

Him and love people. He wants us to treat people the way we would want to be treated. If you have done that, you have done your best.

I'm excited about how healthy your brain is becoming. You are learning how to think like the Bible tells us to think. The Bible is filled with the blessings of God and we have so much to learn from it. Great job digging in to learn it and apply it to your life today.

*Let's say our verse together out loud. "There is therefore now no condemnation (Now, you) for those who are in Christ Jesus (now you)."

*Great job! Now say it three times with your loved one out loud.

*Talk with your loved one about the difference between condemnation and conviction.

(Remember, conviction is from God; condemnation is from the devil.)

*Share Time!

*Thanksgiving time!

*Prayer Focus: Pray with your loved one and ask God to show you how to not feel guilty for things that you cannot control. Thank Him for helping you to make right choices with things that you can control.

*Let me pray for you. Dear Lord, we love you so much. Thank you for a great day. God, thank you for keeping us in perfect peace. Bless my friend. Bless my friend's family. Thank you that my friend and my friend's loved one are working so hard to learn the Bible, apply it to their lives and to be so peaceful all of the time just like you want us to be. Thank you, Jesus. We love you. In Jesus' name, amen. Sweet dreams, my precious friend!

It's great to be a kid!

Joy Builder #9

Where and When Are We Safe?

"The name of the Lord is a strong tower; the righteous man runs into it and is safe." Proverbs 18:10 ESV

Sometimes we have lists in our heads of places and things that make us feel safe. Maybe before we can go to bed, we even have a certain prayer we feel like we have to say or we have a certain blanket that we need to feel protected, a special teddy bear or a certain amount of light on. We have habits. Not all habits are bad but when we have a habit that we have developed and then something changes and that habit is messed with, we may feel some anxiety.

I remember every night I would yell to my Daddy to tuck me into bed and rub my back until I could fall asleep. I would yell over and over until Daddy would come up, "Daaaaddyyyy!, Daaaaddyyyy!" My poor sister, Annie would get so annoyed at me; but I couldn't relax until my Dad would come in. I had developed a habit. The only thing about habits like this is when Daddy had to work late or had a dance he had to play (because he was a musician) or was away with business, I struggled getting to sleep.

We have to learn to trust God with our safety because guess what? God never sleeps. God never works late. God never has to be out of town. God is always there for us so wherever, whenever, however, we need Him He is able to be there for us.

Maybe it's not even nighttime that you feel unsafe. Maybe it's at school, or the babysitters, or even sleeping over at another friend's house. We can feel nervous and unsafe sometimes at places that are not our homes. In those times we need to remember that we are not alone, God goes everywhere we go. Is that hard for you to believe? That's ok, because it sometimes takes a while for us to remember that we are never alone. Jesus loves us too much to leave us alone. He is such a good God.

Proverbs 18:10 says; "The name of the Lord is a strong tower; the righteous man (or woman) runs into it and is safe." Wow, this says that all we need to do is call on the name of Jesus and we will be safe. Do you believe that is true? Well, yes, the entire bible is truth. You never have to question that. God's Word is 100% truth. The Word says; the name of the Lord is so helpful to us, that when we call on His name, it is like we are running and hiding in a safe tower. That's so cool.

Close your eyes. Have you ever played hide and seek? If you play like we used to play, we had a thing we called "safe". Maybe it was a tree, or the side of a shed or something. If you got to touch "safe", you couldn't get tagged out. The name of Jesus is pretty much our "safe". Picture a place or an event that sometimes makes you feel anxious. Now call out "Jesus!" Go ahead, call it out! Good job. Well, now whenever you have to go through a situation where you don't feel 100%safe, you can trust that Jesus is with you (so you aren't alone), and when you get nervous, you can just call, "Jesus" and He will take away your fear. Pretty amazing, right?

Never be afraid to call out "Jesus!" His name is powerful, and so are you, because remember, you have The Holy Spirit living on the inside of you. Our God loves us so much that He made a way to calm our fears simply by allowing us to open our mouths and say; "Jesus".

---

*Let's say today's scripture together out loud. "The name of The Lord is a strong tower (Now, you)…the righteous man or woman runs into it and is safe" (Now, you) Great job!

*Now say it three times out loud with your loved one.

*What word can we say when we start to feel unsafe anywhere or anytime?

*Share time!

*Thanksgiving Time!

*Prayer Focus: Tonight, pray with your loved one about whatever you shared together and ask God together to help you to never forget to call on the name of Jesus when you feel afraid.

*I want to pray for you. Heavenly Father, we come to you in Jesus' name. Jesus' name is the name that is above any other name. His name is powerful. We thank you that when we are scared or nervous, no matter what it is or where it is, we can say the name Jesus and you will calm our fears. Thank you, God for that power. We love you. Bless my friend. Help my friend to keep growing more and more in love with you and with your Bible, God. Thank you for the name of Jesus. Good night God, amen.

Good night, sweet friend. You are powerful and strong!

Joy Builder #10

Do The Opposite!

"Though an army should encamp against me, my heart will not fear; though war should rise against me, in this will I be confident." Psalm 27:3 MEV

I do not enjoy going to the dentist. Do you? Some people really like it, but I don't. But going to the dentist is good for me, so I go to the dentist. I really love donuts, but, they aren't good for me, so I only eat donuts once in a while and I eat fruits and vegetables every day, because they help to make me healthy. I don't like doing sit-ups, but if I don't do sit ups, my pants don't fit the way I want them to fit, so I do sit-ups. I don't love sorting laundry, doing laundry, folding laundry and putting laundry away, but my family needs clean clothes to wear, so I do laundry every day.

What point am I trying to make here? I do the opposite of what I want to do sometimes because it is God's best for me. We need to do the same with our anxiety. We may have something that we are really afraid of doing. Maybe we are afraid of trying a new health food, flying on a plane, or taking that new class at school that the teacher suggested for us because we are really smart. Sometimes any type of change or first time doing something makes us really scared. This is normal, but it's not God's will for us.

God wants us to be adventurous. He has made such amazing people in this world to create inventions that can bring such joy to our lives. For example, God created someone to build the first roller coaster, and wow, roller coasters are fun! Do you like them? If you don't, I bet it's because you have never ridden one before or maybe one you rode on wasn't that great. But, truly, roller coasters are so much fun, and in order to enjoy them, we have to just hop in line and fight our fear and step on and buckle up.

God created someone with the idea to build airplanes. Airplanes are amazing. They allow us to get somewhere very far away, very quickly. They are spectacular. But, you might be a little afraid to ride on an airplane. Just as I said before, it's probably because you have either never flown on one or perhaps when you flew you were worried so much, you couldn't enjoy it. Guess what? I Love riding on airplanes. I haven't always loved it, but now I love it because I just made a decision that I was going to push through my fears and enjoy flying.

There are so many things that God has created humans to invent, or God simply created it Himself for our enjoyment, pleasure and well-being, but, our fears try to keep us from enjoying them. Guess what? You don't have to let fear win anymore! It's the truth! Fear does not get to make your choices anymore. Faith does!

I want you to think of something that you are afraid of. Right now, close your eyes and think about it. I bet something has already come to mind. Maybe it's the dark. Maybe you don't like sleeping in a dark room and you have asked your loved one to keep the lights on while you sleep. Let me tell you something, I understand because I really don't love the dark either. But, when I sleep in a dark room, I do not leave a light on or a TV on, I sleep so much better. God designed the dark to help us to sleep well, so we can feel great the next day. The cool thing is; if God created something, it is good and we don't have to fear it.

So, how do we stop fearing what we closed our eyes and thought of? Well, we do it afraid. We make a decision to push through and do what is called opposite action therapy. Those are big words for doing things afraid until we just aren't afraid of them anymore. It's all about faith.

Don't, misunderstand. We should not do things that are dangerous for us. God has given us our trigger remember? Our trigger is that voice inside us that keeps us safe. But, if we are afraid of things that are not supposed to be dangerous for us, we have to overcome these fears by simply doing it afraid a few times, then next thing we know, we aren't afraid of it anymore. It's so awesome!

Let me tell you a story. My niece was on vacation with her family at a resort. They had a fun game out at the pool called karaoke. Have you ever done karaoke? It is so fun. You are given a microphone and a song is played with words on a screen and you sing along to the song by reading the words. I love karaoke.

My niece wanted to do karaoke, but she was afraid of getting up there in front of people and doing it. She loved the songs. She loved singing to them, but her fear kept her from singing the first few days of vacation. By the third day of vacation, she made a decision to stand up there and sing whether she was afraid or not. The video that my sister took was beautiful. My niece was smiling from ear to ear because she had overcome her fear and she was enjoying a fun thing. Fear didn't win this time, faith did. Now, I can bet the next time karaoke is brought out to the pool, or somewhere where my niece is, she will not be afraid to do it, because she practiced opposite action therapy and she pushed through and faced her fear. I'm so proud of her.

This is something we have to do all of the time. Starting a new school year will make us nervous a lot. We begin to worry, "Who will our teacher be?" "Will I have friends in my class?" "Will the kids like me?" The night before the first day of school each year can be a little scary. But, do we stop going to school because of this? Heavens, No! We push through, we get up and we go to school. Before we know it, school is out for the day and we have had an amazing day meeting new friends, learning new things and starting a new year. Each time we push through our fears and walk in faith, we are practicing opposite action therapy. We have to do this with new things a lot. It's a good thing. It helps us grow and makes us courageous.

Remember I had you think about that one thing that makes you nervous? Right now, ask your loved one if this thing is good for you or bad for you. If it is good for you, I want to encourage you to make a plan to do it afraid for the first time and push through that fear in faith. If it is bad for you, then good job using good judgment. Stay away from bad things, and listen to your trigger. Go ahead and ask your loved one right now.

---

*Let's practice our scripture together two times: Psalm 27:3 (MEV):"Though an army should encamp against me, my heart will not fear; though war should rise against me, in this will I be confident." Great job. Let's say it again

Psalm 27:3 (MEV):"Though an army should encamp against me, my heart will not fear;
though war should rise against me, in this will I be confident."

*Great. Now say it again with your loved one. I'm so proud of how many scriptures you are learning. The Word of God is the sword that you need to always have ready to fight anxiety. Great job.

*So, are you a little nervous about that one thing that you are going to try to do afraid? I totally understand. But, remember, opposite action therapy works. We all have to do it sometimes. You are becoming so courageous.

*Is there another thing that you can remember doing afraid and now you aren't afraid of it anymore?

*Share Time!

*Thanksgiving Time!

*Prayer Time: Spend some time in prayer with God asking Him to help you to face your fears head on, to do that one thing afraid and push through in faith.

*Ok, let me pray for you. Dear God, in Jesus' name I pray for my friend. What an amazingly courageous friend I have, who is dedicated to fighting anxiety and fear once and for all. God, please help my friend push through fear and practice opposite action therapy. This is going to take faith God and lots of help from you. Help my friend. God, you are so good to us. Bless my friend with peaceful sleep. Bless my friend with great dreams. Help my friend to dream about superheroes, because my friend is becoming a superhero fighting anxiety every day. We love you, God. We thank you, God. We are grateful for your love. In Jesus' name! Amen.

Wow, I have such faith in you! You are becoming so strong. Sleep sweet.

Laughter is good medicine!

Joy Builder #11

I Don't Want to Think About Me Today!

"Is it not to share your food with the hungry and to provide the poor wanderer with shelter- when you see the naked, to clothe him, and not to turn away from your own flesh and blood? Then your light will break forth like the dawn, and your healing will quickly appear; then your righteousness will go before you and the glory of the Lord will be your rear guard." Isaiah 58:7-8

My sweet friend, did you know that helping other people actually helps us to heal when we hurt? Science and doctors have done studies which show that when we reach out and help people who are in need, our bodies actually release different things that make us feel good. A couple names for these things are dopamine and endorphins. Those are silly words, right? But, they are really good words. These words are what scientists use to explain why our bodies react in a really good way when we do nice things for others or we bless others with money or things.

Have you ever cleaned out your closet and given toys to some kids who don't have any toys? At Christmastime, has your mom said to you; "Let's give some of these things away so we can make room for your new gifts"? When you actually drop off those toys for needy people, how do you feel? Good, right? That's because you are helping others and it makes your body feel good all over to do that.

I love helping people. I love to find people that are hurting and try to help them. I am not joking when I tell you that I feel so good after I have worked really hard on a project for Jesus helping someone else. I feel healthy, happy and blessed. It is such a magical feeling. Guess what? God made our bodies to feel good when we do good things. God is so cool! That's why this scripture today says that if we help the hungry or give someone food or shelter when they need it, our healing quickly appears. God made our bodies to literally heal when we help people.

I can honestly tell you that the best healing I have received for my anxiety has been by learning to live my life loving and helping other people. It's my favorite thing to do. I think it is when I feel the best. Sometimes when I am so dirty and tired from cleaning up a yard for a widow (a widow is a lady who's husband died), giving food to homeless people, helping a single mom by babysitting for her or even carrying and sorting food for our food pantry that when I am finished and I take a shower, it's almost like God poured His love all over me and I feel so close to Him. God truly, truly loves when we reach out to help other people. He loves it so much, that Jesus said in the Bible, "It is more blessed to give than to receive." Guess what that means? It means that the person giving the gift or the person that is doing the helping gets even more blessed by God than the person that receives the stuff. Isn't that neat?

Do you think that you could think of some place that you could serve someone and help them? Is there somewhere at your church or your school or maybe even at a community group that you could find something that you could do to be a blessing to someone else? I bet your loved one would love to help you find somewhere to serve. I want to challenge you to try. I can almost promise you, after you get home from volunteering, you will feel so good inside you will not have any anxiety that day. Does that sound great or what?

Helping other people helps us. Getting our minds off ourselves and on helping other people heals us. Being a blessing to other people, opens up a chance for God to bless us. Let's give it a try.

---

*Let's say our verse together. It's a long one, but a good one. "Is it not to share your food with the hungry (Now, you) and to provide the poor wanderer with shelter (Now, you) when you see the naked, to clothe him, and not to turn away from your own flesh and blood? (Now, you) Then your light will break forth like the dawn (Now, you) and your healing will quickly appear (Now, you) then your righteousness will go before you and the glory of the Lord will be your rear guard."(Now, you)

Great job! That was our longest scripture reading yet and you did so well with it. I have to admit, it's one of my favorites, because you know I love to serve God by helping people.

*Now say it out loud two more times with your loved one.

*What do you think you could do to help someone else? Where could you serve and be a blessing?

*Can you make a point to set a time with your loved one to serve somewhere together?

*Share Time!

*Thanksgiving Time!

*Prayer Focus; Ask God to show you where or who you could serve. Thank Him for the chance to be able to show God's love to the world through serving others.

*Can I pray for you? Dear Heavenly Father, we come to you in the healing name of Jesus. We love you so much. You are so good to us. You have blessed us with so many things and loved ones. Help us to find somewhere to be a blessing to other people. Help my friend to find somewhere to serve and God, when my friend is serving, bless my friend and make my friend's mind and body feel so good. You are so cool, God. Thanks for making our bodies so awesome. In Jesus name, amen.

Well my friend, get some sleep. You will need your energy when you find where you are going to serve God. I love you. Good night.

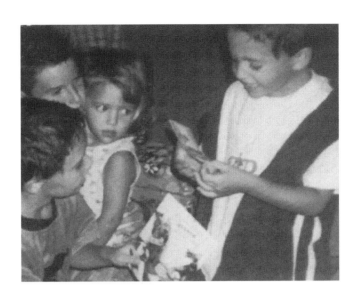

Joy Builder #12

Bullies Aren't Tougher Than Jesus

"...and do not give the devil a foothold" Ephesians 4:27

Have you ever been bullied by someone? Has anyone ever tried to get you to do something by using force or a mean attitude or words? I remember being bullied a couple times growing up by some very insecure girls. It is a terrible feeling and I remember a couple of those times wanting to avoid school or the place I would see them because I thought that would make it stop. Thank goodness my mom wouldn't let me skip school because of a mean person. She made me do what I am going to tell you to do right now: Stand up to that bully.

Bullies don't stop bullying unless they realize they aren't going to get away with it. If you are being bullied by another child, or even an adult, you need to stand up to those bullies by letting your loved one know so your loved one can report those children to the teacher or report the adult to their authority to make the bullying stop. It never helps to just run from the bully. You have to stand up to them by making them accountable to rules. God doesn't want you bullied. He loves you too much.

Anxiety is a type of bully. We have to be very serious about not just running away and trying to hide from things that scare us or give us irrational fears. (Irrational fears are fears that don't make sense to anyone but us.) I'm telling you this so that you can break the strength of that bully called anxiety. If something scares us and we are so afraid of it that we try to avoid it altogether, we have to first ask: Is this thing dangerous or am I just worried it will become dangerous?

 Remember, sometimes our trigger will make us know something is dangerous and we should avoid it for our safety, like playing on a bridge or walking out in traffic without looking, or touching a hot burner on the stove. Our trigger protects us. However, if we begin to be afraid of things that shouldn't scare us, we need to realize that we have to stand up to it so it can't make us afraid of something else. In a way, it's like a bully.

One way we can stand up to the bully anxiety is by doing what I call opposite action therapy. That's a couple big words that mean you face your fear head-on. Suppose you become afraid of fishing. Since fishing is really something fun to do, we know it's not our trigger that is making us afraid of it, so it must be our anxiety. The best thing you can do to avoid making yourself be bullied by a fishing - anxiety bully is to make a plan and go fishing with your loved one or friend. Even though you might feel afraid doing it that first time, you will not let that anxiety intimidate you and you won't be afraid of it again.

Maybe you are afraid of flying in an airplane. The best thing that you can do to avoid letting an airplane anxiety bully get to you is to go on an airplane, whether you feel afraid of it or not. Then, after you have flown once or a couple times, you will turn around and wonder, where did that airplane anxiety bully go? He's gone. This routine works with any anxiety bully. You stand up to them once with your knees shaking and then the next time your knees don't shake. The third time you aren't afraid at all. It's like magic to stomp out anxiety bullying.

Opposite action therapy is very important because if an anxiety bully thinks he won and you stop doing something that could be a blessing to you, the next thing you know anxiety bully will give you another fear. Anxiety bullies are not nice. However, I promise they lose their strength when you stand up to them by doing opposite action therapy and doing it with prayer and calling on Jesus to help you through it. Anxiety bullies have no strength compared to Jesus. Jesus put the powerful Holy Spirit on the inside of you so that you can stand up to any anxiety bully that tries to steal your joy.

Never run away from bullies. Tell a loved one if you feel bullied. Our loved ones will help us. If the bully is anxiety, don't worry. Jesus has you covered. He's got this!

---

*Let's practice our scripture out loud together. It's an easy one, it pretty much means don't give that devil a chance to bully you. Here we go. "Don't give the devil a foothold."(Now, you) Great job.

*Now say your scripture out loud two more times with your loved one.

*Are you being bullied by anyone or have you ever been bullied by anyone? How do they make you feel? If so, tell your loved one right now so they can help you.

*From today on I want you to practice opposite action therapy with any anxiety bullies you may have.

*Share Time!

*Thanksgiving Time!

*Prayer Focus: Talk to God and ask Him to show you how to stand up to your anxiety bullies by doing exactly that thing that is trying to scare you. Thank God for your trigger so you know to avoid dangerous things that God may be protecting you from.

Let me pray for you. Dear God, it's been a long day. It's time for my friend to rest my friend's body and brain so my friend can be healthy and happy tomorrow. Help my friend to get an amazing night's sleep and wake up ready to face an awesome day with You! Thank you, Jesus, that we are never alone. We love you, Lord. In Jesus' name we pray. Amen.

Good night, my awesome friend. I love you

It Is Written

Jesus answered, "It is written: 'Man shall not live on bread alone, but on every word that comes from the mouth of God.'"
Matthew 4:4

Do you ever read the Bible? Does your loved one read the Bible to you? How about in Sunday school? I love, love, love the Bible. It is like God's guidebook to living this life well. It's not only called the Bible. Sometimes people call it The Word of God. Sometimes we just call it The Word. But, make no mistake about it. It's the best book that has ever been written. How could it not be the best? It was written by God. Well, God gave select people the words to write. The entire Bible is what God spoke to men to have them write it down so people like us could read it and live according to it's contents.

The Bible is not only a love letter from God and a guidebook on how to live, it is also a sword to fight anxiety. Really? A sword? Yes, actually a man named Paul in the Bible calls it "The Sword of the Spirit." Wow! We have a sword in our hands to fight evil, to fight the devil, to fight fear, to fight sickness, to pretty much fight anything that isn't good. Our bibles are our swords to fight our anxiety. Do you get excited about fighting anxiety and winning once and for all? I do. Oh, I love The Bible. Did I say that yet?

I want you to love the Bible too. Do you know why? Because the more you love the Bible, the more you will read the Bible. The more you read the Bible, the more you will memorize the Bible. The more you memorize the Bible, the more you will speak the Bible out loud. The more you speak the Bible out loud, the less you will worry. Pretty cool, right?

We can fight the devil's tricks to try to get us to worry by saying three words that Jesus even said when He fought the devil. Those three words are; "It is written." Can you say that right now? Great job. When the devil attacked Jesus, Jesus would say; "It is written" and He would say a scripture out loud to the devil and the devil would leave. Wow? That's powerful. But, it's only powerful if we know the Word of God. Therefore, we have to learn our Word. Ok?

I want you to say this out loud. "It is written, God hasn't given me a Spirit of fear." Go ahead and say that right now (Praise God, you are really getting good at this). When the devil tries to get you afraid, say out loud; "It is written, God hasn't given me a Spirit of fear." Sometimes you will only have to say it once and the devil will leave you alone. But, sometimes, you have to keep saying it until something truly magical happens and you realize, you aren't afraid. It is the coolest thing, because it is a God thing!

We have to do what Jesus did. We have to quote the Word of God out loud to the devil to get him to be quiet in our head. I say "It is written" all the time because when that devil is trying to steal my peace and ruin my mood, I know I had better pick up my Sword of the Spirit and fight. This is an actual sword that even kids can use, remember, that sword is our bible. We need it to be powerful against anxiety.

Let's say it together one more time, "It is written. God hasn't given me a Spirit of fear." (Now, you) Amazing! How do you feel? Powerful? Good because you are. Remember, you are powerful because you have Holy Spirit living on the inside of you. Now you have Holy Spirit and your Sword of the Spirit, The Word of God. There's not an anxiety bully that could stand a chance against you now. Praise God. He really does give us what we need.

Well friend, it's up to you to read your Bible and find a few scriptures to fight that devil with. Then, you need to read them, memorize them and say them out loud to the devil when he tries to get you worrying. Take it day by day. We can't memorize the whole bible in one day. We have to go to school and play right? Take it slow, but make sure you are really trying to learn The Word of God. You need it. It's your Sword.

---

*Lets' say our scripture out loud together; "Jesus answered, "It is written (Now, you)"'Man shall not live on bread alone, but on every word that comes from the mouth of God."(Now, you) Amen, great job!

*Go ahead and say it out loud two more times with your loved one.

*What steps can you take to memorize some scriptures?

*Share Time!

*Thanksgiving Time!

*Prayer Focus: Spend some time praying with God and ask Him to give you a love for reading and memorizing the Word of God.

Let me pray for you. Heavenly Father, we come to you in Jesus' name. God, thank you for the Bible. Thank you for giving us a sword to fight the devil. Thank you that your Bible is your love letter to us and a guidebook to live by. God we want to know the Bible better. Help my friend to fall in love with your Word. Help my friend to have an amazing night's sleep. Help my friend to remember that my friend is powerful and loved. We love you God. Thank you for being such a great God. In Jesus' name, amen.

Good night, you amazing warrior! You are so special to me and to God.

Joy Builder #14

All That's Real Is Today

Matthew 6:34

"Therefore do not worry about tomorrow, for tomorrow will worry about itself. Each day has enough trouble of its own."

I love making lists. Do you? I love setting goals and planning for special events and trips. I really get excited about these things. Lists make me happy. I love writing down all of my chores each day. Then as I do each chore, I put a check by them and it makes me feel so good. But, sometimes all of my planning and preparing can get out of hand. Sometimes my brain tries to figure out things that might happen and when those things aren't good things, they make me nervous and I feel anxious.

Do you ever worry; "what if this happens?" or "what if that happens?" I know my brain tries to go there, but I just don't let it anymore. Do you know why? Because Jesus tells us in the bible to not worry about tomorrow. We are supposed to focus our thinking on today, because today is really the only thing we have control over.

Does this mean we don't plan or set goals for tomorrow? No! That's all good stuff. But, when our thinking trails off into thinking about specific situations and how they will turn out in the future, if it isn't making us feel good, then God wants us to stop thinking about it. If we are thinking about the future, and we are daydreaming about good things; then that's ok; that's using our wonderful imaginations that God gave us. But, we have to make sure that we don't let our imaginations steal our peace and focus on scary future situations that will probably never happen, because that is a waste of time and it makes us feel bad.

God gave me a rhyme one time that I want to share with you. Do you like rhymes? I do. They help me to remember things. God said to me; "Trust and obey, all that's real, is today." Can you say that? "Trust and obey. All that's real is today." You see, we really have no control over tomorrow. Only God knows what will happen tomorrow, so we need to not trust Him with it. Also, our yesterdays have already passed. We can't get them back and we don't need to feel bad over and over about maybe something that we did wrong or something that bothered us in the past. If we ask God to forgive us of our mistakes of yesterday, then God forgives us immediately and we need to let yesterday go and focus on today.

Yes, trust and obey all that's real is today. So, if we need to focus on right now in today; what do we focus on? It's simple. We focus on trusting God and obeying Him. Trusting God with whatever may come our way today and obeying anything our Holy Spirit tells us to do today. Trusting God and obeying Him with whatever we face each day keeps us in perfect peace.

God pours His grace power out over us to help us with our specific daily needs. God is a God of today! And, guess what? It's always today right? Today is today, so we need to trust God and obey Him… today.

So, next time you feel yourself start to worry, next time you realize that your mind is making you feel anxious or out of peace, take a second to think about what you are worrying about. Is it something that you are doing right now? Probably not, because usually most of our worries are about past events or future events. If the thing that you are worrying about had to do with yesterday or tomorrow, I want to challenge you to say out loud; "In the name of Jesus, I will stop thinking about this, I will trust and obey, all that's real is today."

You may have to say it a few times. That's ok. Before you know it, you will feel peaceful.

"Trust and obey, all that's real is today!"

_____

*Let's say our scripture together out loud: "Therefore, do not worry about tomorrow. Tomorrow will worry about itself. Each day has enough trouble of it's own." (Ok, now your turn…) Great job!

*Go ahead and say it out loud two more times with your loved one.

*What will you say out loud next time you recognize that you are worrying about the past or the future? (Hint…it rhymes)

*Share time!

*Thanksgiving time!

*Spend time in prayer with God and thank Him that you only have to take this life one day at a time, trusting and obeying Him.

*Let me pray for you. Heavenly Father, I come to you in Jesus' name. I pray for my sweet friend to have an amazing night's sleep focusing only on things that we can control; trusting you and loving you today. I pray for sweet dreams, a restful night and a healthy body as my friend wakes up tomorrow to start a wonderful new day with you. In Jesus' name, Amen.

Joy Builder #15

You Are Loved

"There is no fear in love. But perfect love drives out fear."

1 John 4:18

Do you know that God loves you more than any other person in this world could ever love you? Does that sound crazy? Well, it's the truth. God loves us so much that He sent His Son to die for our sins so that when we die we can live with Him forever. Why did He do this? Because of love and love alone.

God is love, and love is God. Do you know that you could look in the Bible and anywhere that you see the word "love", you could substitute it for "God" and it would work? Also, anywhere that you see the word "God", if you substitute the word "love" that would work. Why? Because our God is a loving Father, and He loves us more than we can even say in words.

We have to realize how much God loves us because when we know how much we are loved, we realize that we really have nothing to fear. Yes, we will have tough days, we will have new scary situations that we will have to walk through; but knowing we are loved helps us to stay in peace in those situations. The Bible says; "Perfect love drives out fear." What that really means is, when we realize how loved we are and we realize that our "Daddy God" is watching over us and that He has the power to fix anything that we are worried about, our fears go away. It's almost like our fears vanish into thin air when we remember we are loved by our "Daddy". That's who God is, you know? He is your "Heavenly Daddy". Sometimes we forget that and we just can't because this helps us feel safe.

Close your eyes. Picture God up in heaven right now turning on a heavenly nightlight so that He can keep an eye on you all night long. Because that really is what God is doing, watching over us. He is our parent that reigns over the whole Universe. The Bible says; God never sleeps. He doesn't sleep and He never gets tired. No, God doesn't even need a night lite. He is full of light so there is no darkness around Him. He is just so amazing. We can't even begin to figure out God.

Aren't you so happy to know that you are loved? Let me explain something. God's love doesn't even have any rules attached to it. He loves us if we are big and He loves us if we are little. He loves us if we are white and He loves us if we are black. He loves us when we are happy and He loves us when we are sad. He loves us when we behave and He loves us when we sin. He doesn't have any rules attached to His love. He just loves us. The best news is that is that there is nothing we can ever do to get God to take away His love. Nothing at all! He will never stop loving us. Wow, we have a great Daddy don't we?

If perfect love drives out fear, we have to remember that God loves us so fear can stay far away from us. When you begin to fear, I want you to say out loud; "No! perfect love drives out fear and I am loved." That's what we have to remind ourselves every day. Sometimes you will have to say it a few times, but I promise, if you close your eyes and say, "perfect love drives out fear" enough times, fear will go away. It's another one of God's miracles that He does. He chases fear away with His love.

*Let's say our scripture together out loud two times: "There is no fear in love. But perfect love drives out fear." There is no fear in love. But perfect love drives out fear."

*Great job, now say it on your own. Wow! You are getting so good at saying your scriptures.

*Here's a question: When does God love us?

*Here's another question: Can we do anything to get God to take His love from us?

You are so smart!

*Share Time!

*Thanksgiving Time!

*Spend time in prayer with God and thank Him for His love for you.

* Let me pray for you: Dear Daddy, we love you so much. But our love for you can't even compare to how you feel about us. There is just no comparison. God, please bless my friend and help my friend to never- no, never, question that my friend is loved by you. Help my friend to feel your love, Lord, tonight. Help my friend to sleep peacefully and have amazing dreams filled with love, love and more love. In Jesus' name, I pray, Amen!

Sleep tight, sweet friend! God loves you and so do I!

Joy Builder #16

A Wall of Word

"These commandments that I give you today are to be on your hearts. Impress them on your children. Talk about them when you sit at home and when you walk along the road, when you lie down and when you get up. Tie them as symbols on your hands and bind them on your foreheads." Deuteronomy 6:6-8

In my bedroom I have an entire wall where I paste scriptures that I have written on index cards. I write them in different colors. I do some in cursive and I type some, print some and highlight some. I just love looking at the Word while I lay in bed, or while I curl my hair or while I get dressed for the day. I put the Word everywhere around me because The Word is healing for my anxiety and it keeps me at peace. I love going into my room to pray and looking up to focus on God's Word sometimes to see what His Word says about some things that I am talking to God about. It is my goal to memorize and place in my heart many truths from the Bible so there is no room for lies from the devil. The more truth that we focus on, the happier we are.

Truths like: "There is no fear in love, but Perfect love drives out fear."

Truths like: "Cast all of your cares on me because I care for you."

Truths like: "Jesus Christ came to save sinners."

Truths like: "Jesus came so that we may have peace."

Truths like: "Trust in the Lord with all of your heart."

Truths like: "Fear not, I am with you."

All of these truths are written on index cards on the wall near my bed so that I can remember them. You see, I am human and I forget things sometimes and I have to be reminded. So do you. We can't just think, *Oh, I'll just remember these scriptures. I don't need to write them down."* The truth is; just as your teachers in school tell you to write down your assignments so that you don't forget them, you need to write down God's Word so that you don't forget it.

Maybe you can start a wall of Word! You definitely have to ask Mom and Dad or your loved one first. Maybe they will buy you a poster board to put your scriptures on, or an art canvas. You could get really creative. It doesn't matter what you make it look like, it just matters that it is somewhere that you can see it every day and somewhere that you can go when you need to be reminded of truths.

I love my wall of Word. I keep adding to it because I keep finding more and more of God's Word that I love and want to write down. I hope you love making yours too.

 *Let's just say part of this long scripture together. It's talking about God's truths. "Talk about them when you sit at home and when you walk along the road, when you lie down and when you get up." Let's say it two more times together.

"Talk about them when you sit at home and when you walk along the road, when you lie down and when you get up" "Talk about them when you sit at home and when you walk along the road, when you lie down and when you get up."

*Ok, try to say it on your own now. Great job! You are a biblical scholar in the making!

*Why do we need the Word where we can see it?

*Ask your loved one if you could make a Wall of Word. Look around your room and pick where you will put it.

*Share time!

*Thanksgiving Time!

*Spend time in prayer with God and ask Him where He wants you to put your Wall of Word and ask Him what scripture to start with.

*Let me pray for you right now. Dear God, I come to you in Jesus name and I thank you for my friend. I thank you that my friend is learning your Word and learning that we can cast our cares on You, Jesus. I thank you that Your Word is truth. Help my friend to memorize, memorize, memorize scriptures and fall in love with Your truths. In Jesus' name, Amen!

Joy Builder #17

Do You Believe In Miracles?

"You are the God who performs miracles, you display your power among the peoples." Psalm 77:14

Do you believe in miracles? I do and so does Jesus! I have seen God do so many amazing miracles. I cannot even begin to tell you how cool it has been. I want to share with you a few things that God has allowed me to see.

I have seen God heal my kids when they don't feel well and I lay hands on them and pray for healing. I have seen God whisper to me on a walk to go introduce myself to one of my neighbors, she invited me in and we prayed together and her son who was having seizures stopped having them that day. I have seen God heal my sister, who was in a car accident, of countless broken bones including her neck that healed in 10 days. It was so amazing.

I have seen God make it rain on all of my neighbors except me because we were outside painting our house asking God to hold off the rain until we finished. Then the second we finished, it downpoured. I have seen God hold off the rain for a church picnic because our Pastor prayed that He would.

I have seen God give me all green lights when I prayed for them when I was running late to a work event. I have seen God allow us to coast miles on no gas, up and down hills with the engine totally off as we prayed for Him to get us to a gas station with our family. I have seen God tell me, "check the oil" on my son's car only to find it was bone dry and should have completely blown the engine, but it didn't, while I bought oil for him to put in.

I have seen God allow me to lose a bag while shopping so that I had to go back to the store to look for it, only to find a friend see me there and say, "Oh my goodness Mo, I can't believe you are here. I prayed and God told me to call you, I didn't even have to. He put you right in front of me." If I hadn't lost that bag, I would have left by then. And of course, God is so good, I went back and the bag was right there waiting for me. He cares about the littlest details.

I have seen God perform amazing miracles in ministry in which He would send the perfect volunteer at the perfect time to do the perfect task, both here in America and on mission trips that we have taken to different countries. In Haiti, Jesus showed me His face twice in a vision.

I have seen God have a friend send me a note of encouragement to say exactly what I needed to hear at the time to encourage my writing. Sometimes, even as I am typing and they say something like, "I don't know why God had me send this but..."

I have seen God do miracles. Is it because I am someone special to Him? Nope! God loves me but He doesn't love me any more than He loves you. God doesn't have favorites. He is a good Daddy. God is simply a God who does miracles. That's how he operates. He isn't like us. We can't do miracles, but the coolest thing is He lets us be part of His miracles sometimes.

I believe that God wants to do miracles with your fears and worries. He doesn't want us worrying, He wants us trusting. He doesn't want us anxious, He wants us praying. He doesn't want us running from things that are scary, He wants us standing up to them and not letting them control us. Our amazing Lord Jesus wants to heal our anxiety.

Here is the only rule to God's miracles. We have to believe! You see, God won't do miracles for people who won't believe in what He did. God has allowed me to see many miracles because I believe in every one of them. I know it isn't a coincidence. I know it isn't random things that happen. I know it is miracles. And, I think I will continue to see more and more until I go to Heaven someday because I expect God to do it. I think that kind of expecting and believing makes God smile.

Will you believe for a miracle with me tonight? I hope you will.

*Let's say our scripture together two times; ""You are the God who performs miracles, you display your power among the peoples." ...Awesome, let's say it again. "You are the God who performs miracles, you display your power among the peoples."

*Praise God! Now go ahead and say it on your own to your loved one. You can do it!

* Have you ever seen God do a miracle? Tell your loved one all about it? If not, do you want Him to? What kind of miracle would you pray for?

*Share Time!

*Thanksgiving Time!

*Prayer Time: Spend time in prayer asking God to do a miracle with your anxiety and help you to overcome something that you have been afraid of for a while.

*Now I want to pray for you. Heavenly Father, you are a good Father to us. We are so thankful for you. Thank you for my friend's courage to ask for a miracle from you. I don't know what my friend asked for but you do God. I know you do and I know you can perform that miracle for my friend. Help my friend to sleep so peacefully, Lord, so that my friend can wake up tomorrow ready to conquer the day with You. I love you God, you are so good. In Jesus' name I pray, Amen.

Joy Builder #18

Take Care of Your Temple

1 Corinthians 6:19

Do you not know that your bodies are temples of the Holy Spirit, who is in you, whom you have received from God?

Do you like fruits and vegetables? I do, but I haven't always liked them. When I was little I liked donuts and cookies more than I liked fruits and vegetables but my mom would make me eat them sometimes to stay healthy. I didn't understand this as a kid, but it makes sense to me now as a mommy. When my children were little I would say, "Three fruits a day!" They were not allowed to have any junk food until they had eaten at least 3 fruits that day. Why? Because I love them. Mommies and daddies want what is best for their children. We want them healthy, growing and strong.

Mommies and daddies know that fruits and vegetables make our bodies work right. Not true with donuts and cookies.

God is serious about us taking care of our bodies. He wants us healthy because He loves us. He also wants us to remember that when we made Jesus Lord, the Holy Spirit came to live on the inside of us. We carry God around on this inside of us and He doesn't want to live near junk. He wants to live in a healthy body. We need our bodies healthy so we can do the work that God wants us to do for Him.

What is that work? Our work that we do for God is loving God and loving people and telling people about God. That's it! If we are sick and tired because we ate bad food, didn't sleep well or hadn't exercised, we will have a hard time wanting to do any work for anyone. We will just want to lay around and be lazy. Of course some days, we are allowed to be lazy. But, as a whole, we need to keep our bodies active and moving so we feel well.

What does this have to do with worry? Well, the truth is; sometimes not taking care of ourselves can make us not think correctly. Do you know that too much caffeine will make you anxious? It does me. I can't have any caffeine in the afternoon at all or I have a hard time sleeping and I am pretty edgy in the evening. What is caffeine? It's a chemical that is in some sodas and chocolate and even coffee. You may notice that if you have caffeine with dinner, you will struggle sleeping that night. Oh, and sleep is so good for us. We have to get a good night's sleep so God can reset our bodies for the next day.

Do you know if you eat too much junky food, or if you don't exercise or take your vitamins sometimes you may feel depressed? What is depressed? It means that we feel sad and we don't know why. We have to eat three square meals a day and healthy snacks in between as well as drink lots of water for our bodies to perform the way God made them to perform. Healthy food gives us energy, water keeps our body cleaned out the way it should and exercise gives our brains certain natural chemicals it needs to feel happy.

Do you know that we should go outside every day to play? Even if it is for a little while. The sun gives us vitamin D and vitamin D makes us feel happy. When we sit inside all day and watch TV or play video games, our body is craving vitamin D and fresh air. If we don't get it, we can feel worried or depressed. Even if we go outside for at least 15 minutes to play, it will help us feel better that day. If it's cold and snowy out, you'd better bundle up. But that's ok. You can build a snowman and that will make you feel very happy too!

Playing with friends, laughing with friends, and spending time watching funny shows or reading funny books is also good for our bodies. God loves when we laugh. He made us to laugh. If we aren't laughing often, we can sometimes feel worried or depressed.

So, isn't it crazy, that maybe we are anxious or afraid simply because we have to take better care of our bodies? But, guess what? It is never too late to start good habits. Here are a few healthy tips.

*Eat at least 3-5 fruits and veggies a day! Your loved one will help you figure out which ones you like.

*Drink a lot of water during the day. Water is the best drink there is. It's really the only drink we ever need.

*Take a multi-vitamin once a day. Your loved one can give you the one they approve of.

*Get a good night's sleep every night. Remember, this is when God resets our bodies for the next day. Eight hours a night is my favorite, but you may need more.

*Exercise every day. You don't have to go to a gym. Exercise can be riding your bike, swimming in your pool, playing kick ball with your neighbors, or even going for a walk with your family. Exercise makes us feel so good.

*Smile and laugh on purpose. Read a funny book or watch a funny movie that your loved one approves of. Laughter is like medicine. It even says so in the Bible.

I promise that I am doing all of these things with you. I love taking care of my body. After all, it's where God lives. ☺

*Let's practice our scripture together two times, "Do you not know that your bodies are temples of the Holy Spirit, who is in you, whom you have received from God?" Great! Let's say it again. "Do you not know that your bodies are temples of the Holy Spirit, who is in you, whom you have received from God?"

*Ok, now you can say it on your own to your loved one.

*What can you do to make healthier choices?

*Why do we need to take care of ourselves?

*Share Time!

*Thanksgiving Time!

*Prayer time: Spend time in prayer with God thanking Him for making your body so perfect. Ask Him to show you what things you can do to live healthier every day?

*Ok, I want to pray for you. Dear God, we come to you in Jesus' name. Lord, we love you. We honor you. We thank you for making our bodies so cool. Thank you for thinking of all of the details to keep us healthy. Help my friend to take great care of my friend's body. Help us to always treat our bodies with respect because it is where Holy Spirit lives. God, help my friend to sleep in peace, have great dreams and wake up reset to start tomorrow in a great mood and with a powerful Spirit. In Jesus' name, Amen.

Good night, my friend! Stay healthy!

Joy Builder #19

Maybe You Are Mad

"In your anger do not sin. Do not let the sun go down while you are still angry," Ephesians 4:26

Does your anxiety ever make you mad? Do you get frustrated because people don't always understand how you feel? I get it! I remember when I was frustrated so many times with my husband because he didn't understand why I felt like I needed to keep checking on things I already checked on, like to make sure the stove and curling iron were off when I left the house. You see, sometimes we get angry because we have been hurting for a long time. I want you to remember something: anger isn't bad, but acting out in anger is bad. We just have to learn how to voice our anger without hurting others or breaking rules because of our anger. Does that make sense?

I remember when my daughter Sara was three and I took her to a swimming class. This was a special swimming class so that she could survive if she ever fell in the water. It was called "Survival Swimming", but it was not easy. This class was every day for a couple weeks, for ten minutes a day. The first day, Sara was excited. She didn't know how hard she would have to work at this class, so she was happy about it. But the second day she was not as excited and she wanted me to let her quit. She cried the whole way to the swimming instructor's house and, even though it made me sad, I kept telling her, "Sara, this is so good for you, you are going to be swimming in no time and it will protect you from harm." But, Sara did not listen, she just kept crying and asking me to go back home. Though it made me feel really sad, I knew I had to help her push through because it was a healthy thing for her.

Once we arrived at the instructor's house, Sara's fear turned to anger. I still remember Sara running around the pool saying as many bad words as her little three year old mind had learned at this point. She misbehaved, ran from me, then when I finally put her in the pool with the instructor she scratched the teacher so badly, the teacher still has a scar there today. It was a really hard day. But do you know, because we didn't give in to Sara's fear, she was swimming the entire length of the pool at three years old by the end of that week? We talked all the way home about how her behavior was inappropriate, and when we got home she made her teacher a card to say she was sorry. When we returned to lessons the next day, she brought her the card, gave her a hug and never fussed about swim lessons again.

What happened that day? Sara's fear of the class turned to anger because she didn't know how else to voice her fear. I look back and I think that if Sara had just talked to me about her fears of the class, I could have explained what the class was all about. I could have helped her understand and maybe she could have even enjoyed the class instead of dreading it. But she was only three years old and she didn't know how to explain her fears.

Do you ever have a hard time letting your loved one know what you are worried about? Do you keep your worries to yourself? Let me tell you, talking about our worries is so helpful. When you have something that you are worried about, maybe a test coming up in school, or a person that isn't being nice in class or anything, the best thing that you can do is to talk to your loved one about it. Why? Because there is something very healthy about talking about our troubles and not just trying to forget about them and keep them to ourselves. When we keep our fears and worries inside and we don't talk about them it's almost like they grow. They start to make us worry about other things. They also can make us feel sick to our stomachs or give us headaches. Yes, talking about our fears and not letting our fears turn to anger is healthy for us; almost as good for us as eating an apple.

If we can talk about our fears to our loved ones, and allow our loved ones to help us with these fears, which doesn't always mean they will help us avoid our fears (remember, I still made my daughter go to swim lessons even though she was afraid of them), then, we can learn to trust God more as we face our fears quickly, before we become angry.

Does that sound good? Remember, we have to be real to be healed. So make sure you talk to your loved one about whatever you are nervous about tonight. We have to let God shine on our dark thoughts, because once God is allowed to work on our pain our pain has no choice but to go away. God always wins! He's amazing! I love you. I really do.

*Let's practice our scripture together two times:

"In your anger do not sin. Do not let the sun go down while you are still angry."

*Great, let's say it again. "In your anger do not sin" Do not let the sun go down while you are still angry."

*Ok, now you can say it on your own to your loved one?

*Is anger bad?

*What is a good way to handle our anger?

*Share Time

*Thanksgiving Time!

*Spend time in prayer with God. Ask Him to show you areas that you may be feeling angry about and let Him know what you are angry about. Ask Him to help you voice your anger in a healthy way.

*Ok, I want to pray for you. Dear God, we come to you in Jesus' name. God, we love you so much. Thank you for helping us realize that anger isn't bad, it's just important that we don't sin in our anger. Help my sweet friend to learn how to talk about whatever my friend is angry about. Help my friend to talk to you and to my friend's loved one about whatever my friend is worrying about. Thank you that you care so much about us that you listen from Heaven every time we pray. Thank you for answering our prayers. God bless my friend. Help my friend to sleep in perfect peace. In Jesus' name I pray, amen.

Good night, sweet friend! Hope you had an awesome talk with your loved one tonight. You are amazing!

Joy Builder #20

You are never alone!

"I will never leave you, nor forsake you." Joshua 1:5

Guess what? You don't have to be afraid when you are alone anymore because the truth is, you really are never alone. I know what you are thinking. *"What, Mo? I have to be alone at night and in the bathroom and sometimes other places?"* I know you do, but the good news is; once you have accepted Jesus Christ as your Savior, He sends The Holy Spirit to live on the inside of you so that you are truly never alone. The Holy Spirit is our guide, our counselor (pretty cool you have a built in counselor, right?), our protector, our helper and our peace-giver.

God tells us in the book of Joshua and then again in the book of Hebrews that once we have Jesus we have Him for good. He never leaves us. Not even for a second.

We can't make a mistake to make Him leave.

We can't cry too much to make Him leave.

We can't hurt someone's feelings so much that we make Him leave.

We can't do anything to make Holy Spirit leave us once we have asked Him in. He promises to never leave us nor forsake us. That is such a wonderful promise and I think of it anytime that I am home alone. I remind myself, that it's not just me there because God is with me.

So, what? Why is this good news? Well, it's good news because we never have to feel lonely again. We never have to be afraid of the lights off at night again. We never have to worry about something happening to us and no one being there. The Holy Spirit is there, and Holy Spirit looks just like Jesus.

It gives us courage. So many times in the Bible when God calls someone to do something big, the first thing He says to them is, "Fear not, I am with you." Why do you think He does that? Well, because He knows us so well. God made us. He knows that when we do something new or we do something that isn't in our comfort zones, we may get a little scared and we have to be reminded that If God is with us, we can accomplish anything we put our minds to.

Whenever I feel myself start to get nervous about anything, I remind myself; "Mo, you are not alone, you have a big God on the inside of you." Then, next thing I know, I have peace again. It's so amazing. This is simply something that you will have to remind yourself when that little feeling of fear comes over you. If you are alone or just nervous about something, remind yourself about that giant God who lives on the inside of you. Then after you remember that again, enjoy that peace that God wants you to have.

*Say out loud right now, "I am never alone. God is with me." Go ahead and say it again. Great job!

*Now say, "I have a big God on the inside of me!" .....I love it! It's so true.

*When God says, "Never will I leave you, never will I forsake you.", how does that make you feel?

*Let's practice our scripture together two times. "I will never leave you, nor forsake you. I will never leave you, nor forsake you." Joshua 1:5

*Now say it on your own without me. Great job! I'm so proud of you.

*What kind of courageous step could you take knowing that you have a big God on the inside of you?

*Share time!

*Thanksgiving Time!

*Spend time in prayer with God thanking Him that He will never leave you, no matter what. Pray about anything that you shared with your loved one.

*Ok, I want to pray for you. Dear Lord, we love you so much. Thank you for the courage that you give us by reminding us that we are truly never alone. We have you with us every second of every day and every night. Thank you for fighting our battles for us. Thank you for protecting us, guiding us and keeping us safe. Help my friend to never forget that my friend has a big God living on the inside of her/him. Help my friend to sleep in perfect peace. Help my friend to have amazing dreams and wake up refreshed and full of life. We love you and praise you. In Jesus' name, amen.

Good night, my friend! You are courageous! You have a big God on the inside of you. There's nothing you can't do. Love you!

A Letter to My Strong and Courageous Friend

Dear Friend,

Oh my goodness, I am so proud of you. You have worked so hard. Anxiety is a difficult thing to deal with at any age. I know this myself because I have fought anxiety since I was your age. But thanks to Jesus we now know how to fight it, right? We fight anxiety with prayer, the Word of God and telling that ugly bully anxiety to leave us alone in Jesus' name.

Your loved one must be so proud of you. You two studied together, you read God's Word together and some of you even accepted Jesus Christ as your Savior together. That makes me the most happy. Remember that it is so important to find a Bible believing church to attend together as a family. The church is Jesus' design to keep us walking on the right path together as believers in Him. The church is Jesus' bride.

Listen, you aren't done. Even though you worked through all 20 Joy Builders, these Joy Builders are not meant to be a one-time lesson. They are life skills that you learn to live by, practice and work on until they become amazing positive habits in your life. Keep this study by your bed with your Bible and when you struggle with any worries or fears, go straight to the study and remind yourself what to do. It's okay to need reminders as I still remind myself to not worry and to trust God with my life.

Two things that I want you to remember and to never forget is that you can control this and you can never give up. We can't stop fighting. The bible is always there as our sword to fight. It's not going anywhere. God's Word will always be there for us. It's a good idea to hide a lot of scriptures in our hearts though, just in case our room gets too messy and we misplace our Bibles and we need The Word quickly. Hide more and more of God's Word in your heart every day by memorizing scriptures that help you.

Remember to journal. Journaling is like talking to God without our voices. It's so good for us. Remember to put your favorite scriptures up in your bedroom on note cards or however your little artistic heart wants to display them. Remember to talk to Jesus like He is right in the room because friend, He is! He's even closer. He's in your heart. Remember that even when you are somewhere that you can't talk out loud to God, all you have to do is speak to Him in your heart and He will hear you and respond. If you get nervous in school, remember that Jesus came to school with you. If you get nervous anywhere, remember you are never alone. You have the God of the Universe with you. That my friend makes you powerful!

Oh, I could talk to you forever, it makes me happy to encourage you in The Lord, but I have to let you grow up in Jesus on your own. I'm like that mama bird who taught you how to fly and now I have to let you spread your wings. I'm crying right now praying for you. I want you to have so much peace and joy and happiness in your life so that anxiety has no more control over you. That's what I'm praying for you right now.

God has an awesome plan for you. I know this because I know my God and He said it in His Word. I would love to hear how you feel about this book and if it has helped you in any way. Please have your loved one reach out to me on my Facebook page or Twitter and let me know. I want to celebrate your peace with you.

Well, little birdie, go fly! I love you.

Love, Mo

Just For Loved Ones! 10 Tips for Loved Ones of Little Overcomers

1) Less is more with the evening news blaring in the background. Try to protect their ears from too many sad current events.

2) When speaking to other adults about adult issues, be mindful of little ears in the room. If life's struggles get adults uneasy, imagine how it makes kids feel when they do not have the wisdom to properly process these details.

3) A consistent schedule makes all kids feel more secure. Your effort in obtaining a regular eating, sleeping and lifestyle schedule

will help your child in handling other things in life that are out of balance.

4) Swearing and yelling in front of children makes them anxious. When disagreements happen, try your best to discuss them in private away from the children.

5) Sugary snacks, poor food choices and junk food can sometimes cause mood swings with children and adults. Stick to the old fashioned food pyramid when packing lunches for school and preparing meals at home. Junk food is okay once in a while, but remember this tip: *Junk in, junk out. Healthy in, healthy out*

6) When warning children of dangerous things such as strangers, crossing the street, etc, it is best to state that these are dangerous situations, explain to them boundaries and drop it. If you berate your child over and over about danger because of your fear, you could create an unhealthy fear in them. Boundaries and rules are necessary to teach, but do not exasperate them with details over and over.

7) Do not ever speak negatively about your child's other parent, whether married or divorced. This causes anxiety to the child. A united front as parents makes children feel more peaceful.

8) Alcohol and drugs done in front of or around children causes them to feel uneasy. Children like to know what to expect in situations and when parents or others around them are intoxicated they feel out of control of their circumstances. If you are going to partake in alcohol, it is best to have a childcare provider set up for your children. Remember, children should not be involved in adult issues and situations.

9) You will begin to recognize when your Little Overcomer is anxious. It could be nail biting, complaints of a belly ache, or headache, or a blank stare off in the distance. The best questions

that you can ask them are: "Is something bothering you, baby? Want to talk? Talking about our anxiety, breaks anxiety's strength.

10) Keep reminding your Little Overcomer that God has a plan for his/her life and that wonderful plan is why that devil tries to steal his/her joy with anxiety. Remind him/her consistently how loved they are by God.

Peace comes when we learn
to trust God!

Life is Wonderful! Jesus helps us to build more joy each day.

Check out more of Mo's writing and teaching on her website

www.unforsakenministries.com

Made in the USA
Columbia, SC
22 November 2021